TIDES OF Love

TOM CAMPBELL

ISBN 978-1-0980-8729-6 (paperback)
ISBN 978-1-0980-8730-2 (digital)

Christian Faith Publishing, Inc.
832 Park Avenue
Meadville, PA 16335
www.christianfaithpublishing.com

Printed in the United States of America

Introduction

Do you ever wonder what made your husband, wife, or significant other fall in love with you and vice versa? Yeah, I know you are handsome, beautiful, have a great body, make a lot of money, or just in general, you are a cool person with many attributes. But as time goes on and life's intricacies change some of those positives into negatives, it may be difficult to remember all the good things that started you on your path together. Not that you love this person any less, but you may have a hard time remembering all the good times that got your relationship going.

Therefore, every month, I would write a little poem to my wife to help us remember all the different times in our lives.

As you read some of these poems and stories, you will be able to determine that boating and the ocean is important in our lives. This is how the title *Tides of Love* came to be. In our boating life as well as in our on-land life, a person will have many things coming and going, and they will have to adjust to keep "making way" (nautical term for moving on). Many of the poems will reflect things we are about to do, things we have done, situations that go on in our lives like birthdays, anniversaries, or holidays. Not all the poems made it through the cutting room, and I know you will probably think that many of the poems have a familiar ring as to the subject matter and words. As I said, these poems are to my wife about our life, and I did not go back to read what I said the previous month or on a similar occasion from the previous year. The poems are pretty much in order of our life together as it happened.

I added some stories and other things to help you understand us as a couple and how we got together. I know our story is not a unique story by any means, but I hope the words in this book can give anyone a true insight to what our true love is and what anyone's love can be.

Enjoy,
Tom and Nancy Campbell

CONTENTS

A Story of Our Life

We would like to tell you a little story or a list of facts of reality that might help you understand how this beautiful Greek Jewish New York lady could get together with a Scottish Christian redneck Texan. We were brought up in two different cultures and environments, yet our circles of life revolved almost as if they were one, and the number twelve became our number.

I guess the beginning would be our fathers were both named Jesse. Nancy was born at five twenty-five, and I was born at three forty-five. Yes, these numbers add to twelve. I was born on the twelfth month, and she was born on the twenty-first day. Her numbers got reversed, close enough. Nancy was fortunate enough to have a boating life, and this was something that I was only able to think about in my youth. As a child, I saw the movie *Kon-Tiki* and dreamed of sailing across oceans, but I had to be contented with building a raft to float down the bayou near our home in Houston, Texas. Watch out, Errol Flynn, or even Huckleberry Finn. Here comes Captain Tom. Meanwhile, Nancy was standing at the door with her bags packed on a Friday night, waiting for the family to get ready to go to the boat for a weekend of boating and eating deli sandwiches.

Our circles were similar but have not crossed each other yet. In 1976, Nancy bought a yellow sailboat. I also bought a yellow sailboat in that same year. It was an Albin (the same make of boat we have now), so I guess a pattern was being set. Then in July of 1979, Nancy bought a Britton Chance-design sailboat, and as fate would have it, my son was born in that month and year, and I named him Britton Chance Campbell. A little-known fact is that the sailboat designer Britton Chance died on October 12, 2012. The number twelve just keeps popping up. This was getting a little scary.

The saga goes on. By this time in our lives, we were both very much into sailing; and we independently, two thousand miles apart, decided to get our Coast Guard Captain's License. Well, guess what happened in the spring of 1983? Yep! We both got our licenses. In 1998, our paths crossed, and we did not realize it until I let her read one of my articles that had been published in the sailing magazine *Latitudes and Attitudes*. I was on a fifty-four foot charter sailboat in the Tobago Keys in the Windward Islands of the Caribbean. A cruising couple came by our boat asking about the other flag we were flying. Of course, everybody knows the Texas flag, but they were not familiar with the flag of Arkansas, where my friends lived. As it turned out, these cruisers were trading books, video tapes (no CDs in 1998), etc. When Nancy starting reading about the couple Phil and Janie on *Tsolo*, Nancy said she was also there that day doing the trading. She probably would have dropped by our boat with Phil and Janie if she had not been leaving for Trinidad that day. Nancy left at twelve midnight. Whatcha think? A close encounter, and life goes on.

For the next few years, the realities of life dominated our lives. We both worked to reach our goal of going cruising. Nancy was able to fulfill that goal, but I spent several years working in engineering, teaching sailing, doing sailing charters, boat deliveries, and boat repossessions, and I was looking forward to retirement. The bottom line is that our circles of life, our paths, and our destinies finally came together at the Tarpon Bay Yacht Club in Port St. Lucie, Florida. We both moved there in 2008, with both of our lives being consumed with the illness of our respective spouses. In 2012, they passed away just nine days apart.

Nancy had decided to sell her condominium and move to New York, while I played many rounds of golf by myself and sat on the pier wondering what was next. And that being said, our paths crossed.

While taking a walk, I saw Nancy getting out of her car with several bags. At this point in time, I had not ever spoken to Nancy. Even though my sailboat was almost directly across from her sailboat, our paths never crossed. I had only seen Nancy at an occasional party at Tarpon Bay Yacht Club. As I approached her car, I offered to help her carry the bags into her condominium. She started talking about all the things she had to do, and the items she needed to sell or donate. I told her I would buy the golf clubs and went on my way.

A few months went by and not having anyone to play golf with on a regular basis, I asked Nancy if she would like to play. After we played golf and went to dinner a few times, she asked me if I would like to go to St. Lucie Sailing Club Membership party. Her thought process was that I was a nice guy and there are probably some Texas women in the club that she could introduce to me. She then asked me to go to the Sailing Club's Commodore's Ball on the twelfth of January. There is that number twelve again. The location of the ball was on the Intercoastal Waterway. It had a view of the waterway and the sky that could be enjoyed. It was such a lovely evening, and Nancy asked if I would like to walk out on the pier. I am not sure if she grabbed my hand as a symbol of affection, or she just wanted support in case her high heels got caught in a crack on the pier. Either way, this Texas redneck started to feel a little pounding in his ticker. We had been dancing and having a great time, and I felt that something more was happening. About a week later, I asked her to come to my condo where I would prepare her dinner. I believe it was shrimp etouffee. I gave her a glass of wine and told her that I had some strong feelings for her. She drank the wine, stayed for dinner, and she did not run out of the door. And the rest is history.

After that night, we spent more time together, and I started meeting her friends, cousins, and their spouses. I am sure that this was a cultural shock for all. When I said "Ya'll," they probably thought I was talking about the two-mast sailboat yawl, or "fixin' to" (the rest of the country says "about to") was some kind of mechanical procedure, and "Howdy do?" (Texan for "How are you today?") was an inquiry to a television puppet character from the fifties. Likewise, I had to learn that culture is not some sort of aging process for yogurt, Times Square is not a mathematical term, Monet is not a financial medium, Rembrandt is not a tooth whitener, and the circle line is not a bunch of people wrapped around the block waiting for the opening night of a Broadway play. I already knew that Manhattan was not just an adult alcoholic beverage and that subway was more than a sandwich.

Since our paths had definitely crossed, I gave her a promise ring on February 12, and I promised that I will do everything in my power to make her the happiest, most loved, and safest person in the world. I wanted her to feel that I was totally dedicated to her, and I wanted to make her life the greatest it can be. In other words, I had many tests to pass. This was a challenge that I gladly engaged.

Last year, Nancy invited me to spend the summer with her in New York. While we were there, we decided to buy a boat. This was something that we talked about and looked into prior to leaving Florida. We finally decided on a boat in Rhode Island and made a wonderful trip down to Florida. I am sure both of us and others had some reservations about this partnership. It just so happened that the closing date for the boat was August 12 and the Coast Guard documentation number started with twelve. I am not much of a gambler, but this felt right, and I knew that I wanted to be with Nancy for the rest of my life. On the way down to Florida, we stopped in Myrtle Beach in South Carolina, and I bought her an engagement ring, got on my knee, and proposed in front of the jewelry store workers and customers. Since the number twelve was a positive thing in our lives, we decided to name the boat, the "Twelfth of Never" from the song by Johnny Mathis in 1957. The words of this song say everything that I feel in my heart toward Nancy. If any of you do not remember this great song, it goes like this:

> You ask how much I need you, must I explain,
> I need you Oh my darling, like roses need rain.
> You ask how much I'll love you; I'll tell you to,
> Until the Twelfth of Never, I'll still be loving you.
> Hold me close, never let me go,
> Hold me close, melt my heart like April snow.
> I'll love you till the bluebells forget to bloom,
> I'll love you till the clover has lost its perfume,
> I'll love till the poets run out of rhyme,
> Until the Twelfth of Never, and that's a long, long time.

So welcome to our celebration, our beginning as husband and wife. Enjoy the food, beverage, fellowship, and music. Join us as we celebrate this incredibly happy and beautiful occasion. And as they say in the Big Easy (New Orleans), "*Laissez les bon temps roulez*" (Let the good times roll).

Our First Boat: Homeward Bound
Tom Campbell

Taking a boat trip from Rhode Island to Florida through the Intracoastal Waterway is a fantasy that had been thought about by many boaters but experienced by few. The few and the adventurous are probably the same each year, but this was my first time, and the experience covered all spectrums of the imagination. I did not know what to expect, nor could I totally visualize the adventure to come.

Phase 1 of the adventure was procuring a boat. The boat was only something that Nancy and I talked about prior to leaving for our summer retreat in New Rochelle, New York. We only took boating supplies (i.e., gloves, hats, foul weather gear, suntan lotion, and binoculars) for the possibility of crewing with someone for a day or weekend, not taking a boat on a thousand-mile-plus journey.

We looked at a boat in Stuart, Florida, and decided that this style of boat was the one we liked. We thought that possibly in the fall, if I passed all her tests, we might consider looking more seriously for a boat. Since I passed the preliminary test, and we made it to New Rochelle, New York, we started looking at many boats in different marinas, and some boats that were the same make and model as the one in Stuart, Florida. After careful consideration and deliberation, we decided on the Albin 32+2 Command Bridge. All the Albins that we surveyed had strong attributes that we both wanted. It boiled down to boat age, dinghy davits, new refits of equipment, design of the interior, engine make and model, and hard top Bimini to keep us dry and comfortable while steering or relaxing in the command bridge. We finally agreed on the boat that was the youngest age and the longest distance from our homeport in St Lucie, Florida. The boat was in Tiverton, Rhode Island. We needed to equip the boat for the long-distance journey. As you can imagine, we were busy from

August 12 (closing date) until September 15 when we left. There were times that we questioned our sanity. Even after we bought the boat, we continued to look, and nothing makes us smile more than ours. Well, excluding the Hinkley 65 we saw in Hilton Head, South Carolina.

Prior to leaving New York to go south, we made this beautiful journey from Tiverton, Rhode Island to New Rochelle, New York. We studied *Eldridge* (book of tides) to make sure we had favorable tides for the journey. We could not have picked the weather and tides any better. We cleared Point Judith Harbor with clear vision and calm seas and spent the first night in Stonington, Connecticut, and the next night at Norwalk Islands. This was my first taste of what six-foot tides and associated currents can do, and it is wise to read your tide book and study the upcoming weather.

During the month before we left New York, we upgraded several things on the boat, provisioned it with all of the needed items, practiced anchoring and handling the boat, and enjoyed the sights at many of the anchorages in the Long Island Sound area. Then it was time to head south.

With our spirit of adventure, we set out through the East River, Hell's Gate, the Statue of Liberty, and beyond, moving at speeds of five knots faster than our engine could move us thanks to the outgoing tide and current. Our first stop was Sandy Hook on the North Shore of New Jersey. We spent a day at anchor and a couple of days in a slip. We had to wait for weather since our next phase was down the Jersey coast. We traveled fast to get out of rough weather as soon as possible. This meant traveling at fourteen knots and surfing down six-foot waves at a speed of seventeen knots. This was a good test for the boat, first mate, and captain.

Next was Cape May, New Jersey, up the Delaware Bay, through the C and D Canal, and down the Chesapeake Bay. The rough ride at the south end of the bay made for some interesting boat handling; but Norfolk, Virginia, was near, and the Intracoastal Waterway was upon us.

The whole trip down was a trip through past times in most places. Some trees, churches, and hotels dated back hundreds of years. Atlantic City had taken on a different look since I was there in the nineties, and Nancy was in shock since she remembered North and South Carolina along the Intracoastal Waterway as being a wilderness, and now it is wall-to-wall houses and condominiums. They were on land and the barrier islands. Progress seems to be everywhere. Just about everywhere we stopped, we could borrow a bicycle or car, or shopping was within walking distance. It was a trip down memory lane for Nancy, but all the changes took her breath away.

We finally made it to Savannah, Georgia, to put the boat "on the hard"—that's dry storage for any of you nonboaters. Nancy had to get back to Florida for her driver's license renewal, and I had a couple of doctor's appointments.

We will be going back in the springtime to return the boat to the water and continue south, with a stop at Amelia Island for a Marine Trawler Owners Association rendezvous.

The Campbells' Adventures for 2016
Tom Campbell and Nancy Laub-Campbell

Since Nancy is trying to culturize this redneck Texan and trying to get me knowledgeable on some of the finer things of life (which is about to turn me into some big container of yogurt), we started this year with our one-year anniversary on a two-week cruise from Long Beach, California, through the Panama Canal, with stops in Mexico, Central America, and Columbia. This is a trip that I highly recommend. And read David McCullough's book *The Path between the Seas* before you go. This book inspired me to want to take the trip.

Moving along "Culture Road," or better known in the Campbell house as "To be or not to be yogurt," we took a two-week trip on the cruise ship *Queen Elizabeth* around England, Scotland, and a stop in Belfast, Northern Ireland. We saw everything, from where some of the Beatles lived and Penny Lane to archeological digs in the Orkney Islands in Scotland. We also saw cows that were so fat that when their milk came out, it was butter. We did not see the Loch Ness monster even though I made my famous water monster mating call, but we did find the Campbell Clan Calder Family Crest, which I wore on my tuxedo on formal night on the cruise ship. We also toured Portsmouth, England, and visited the boatyards with many of the old sailing ships of days gone by that were there for exploring.

We followed the England-Scotland trip with a two-month drive across America that spanned from Florida to as far west as Idaho and east to New York and back to Florida. The highlights of the trip were a few days in Memphis, Tennessee, to get in tune with blues and jazz music, a visit to Graceland, and a ride on a riverboat. We stayed a week in Colorado with Nancy's cousin and completed the trip west by staying with my sister in Boise, Idaho. The trip back east led us to Yellowstone National Park, Mount Rushmore, and the inprocess monument of Chief Crazy Horse. We went through the farmland of the Midwest and Nancy discovered that a farm in that area of the country can be as big as Manhattan. After a couple of weeks in the city and surrounding areas visiting relatives and friends and doing New York stuff, we made our way south to some friends in Maryland while dodging a hurricane. Then our trip south blessed us with great weather in Myrtle Beach, South Carolina, for a few rounds of golf. The whole trip was blessed with great weather, which made it possible to get about fifteen rounds of golf in during that two-month tour of America.

Between the cruise ship tours and the drive around America, we made several trips in our boat down to the Keys and as far as Charlotte Harbor on the west coast of Florida. Sometimes we'd just make a trip in our boat to Manatee Pocket for a day or two or West Palm Beach for little mini vacations. Our motto is after golf, tennis, cruising on our trawler, sailing on Nancy's sailboat, and taking a cruise ship somewhere, we want to stay busy. Oh, did I forget to tell you about our two-week trip to Texas in December to see my children and grandchildren for Christmas with a stop in the Big Easy for a couple of days of too much food with lots of butter and drinks with an umbrella and a cherry on the top?

All this being said, we are looking forward to a busy 2017. If you are out there, we hope to see you having as much fun as we.

CHAPTER 1

2013

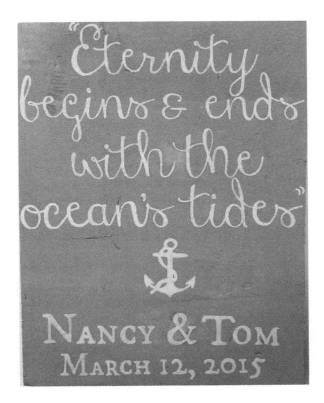

I Thought of You Today

Three months have passed,
And I cannot remember,
Did I fall in love with you today?
Or was it last September.

The day is not important,
Just a place in time,
But when I think of you,
I am thankful you are mine.

From this day forward, and as I pledged before,
With all my heart and soul, each day I will love you more.
The twelfth of each month is the Twelfth of Never,
And this guy promises to love you forever.

OUT ON THE PIER

Was the tide in flood, or was it in ebb?
The breeze was in our face as we walked ahead.
The sounds of the water and the sky were so clear,
Made for a perfect evening, walking out on the pier.

Feelings of past days, we cannot understand,
But something special happened as you took my hand.
We leaned on the railing, it made me want to cheer,
A new feeling came upon me, out on the pier.

If deck chairs had been out there, we could sit and count the stars,
I wonder how many, I wonder how far?
A shooting star must have seen us, never to come near,
But it left a glow around us, out on the pier.

There are these words of a song, so just in case,
They go, "With every kiss and warm embrace."
May this feeling never leave; may it grow with each year,
A bond linked forever that started out on the pier.

Words from the Heart

I was having a wonderful dream, and then sleep came to an end.
I smiled and I sighed, it was time for the day to begin.
The dream was beautiful; it is hard to explain,
I think about its merits, was it real or just insane?

I was smiling and laughing and holding the person that I love,
The feeling that was inside of me could only come from above.
Things that were said, the happiness that we shared,
Oh, what a dream I had, for which I was not prepared.

I grew closer to this person, our hearts became as one,
Nothing else matters, not even the moon, not even the sun.
I stood and I said, "Everything is all right,"
For this was not a dream, it was you, last night.

Take these words, my love, they are real and true,
The words are from my heart, from me to you.
As this day goes by, may these words offer you an array
Of love, hope, and happiness, so for now, have a great day.

OUR FIRST HOLIDAY SEASON

December is here, and our eleventh month has ended,
Ninety-two percent gone, and I believe we have blended.
Our bodies, our minds, our souls are as one,
I know it seems long ago, but sometimes just begun.

We walked and we talked, sharing our past lives,
But a new life has started, so onward we strive.
Building this new life, for new things to be,
For when the past is mentioned, it is you and me.

This holiday season, whether Hanukkah or Christmas,
This is our first together, and we know God has blessed us.
May many more come, with joys and blessings to remember,
The time of celebration and prayer, this month of December.

As we go forward, our love will keep us strong,
Never turning back, repairing what is wrong.
Love is our bond, it will keep us together,
For now and always, until the Twelfth of Never.

CHAPTER 2

2014

Remembering Our Beginning

It was this month, a year ago,
You took me out to dance fast and slow.
The party was great, you thought of giving me away,
I guess you decided we had too much fun that day.

We danced and we talked, and something was there,
Was it the rum and the wine, or was something in the air?
We did not know it then, but our stars were aligning,
All to be exposed later, I could see something was shining.

A beautiful song, a touch, and a glance,
Possibly gave us a purpose, to take another chance.
Hidden thoughts we had, we had put in the back of our minds,
What is the protocol at this point in time?

"She is kind of cute," "He dances very well,"
Our thoughts came and went, none we can tell.
This was our beginning, how lucky we are,
Now we travel as one, sometimes near, sometimes far.

The four seasons have passed; our first year draws near,
We will travel many paths together each and every year.
Our hearts and our bodies are one life to be,
Looking to this same time next year, when you are Mrs. C.

Fulfilling a Mother's Wish

There is this number, three hundred sixty-five, or one year,
The number fulfilled a wish, of your mother dear,
The four seasons have passed, and we are still much in love,
With all the blessings that we have, that are blessed from above.

There you were in all your beauty, and I looked into your eyes,
I knew something was happening, that I could not disguise.
I could not control it; I was not in command,
I knew something was happening that I did not understand.

Was it just a moment in time, or something else to be?
Two people standing on the pier; that was you and me.
I told you of my feelings; I did not hold back,
This was your chance to run if the same feelings you lack.

We grew together, as the sun rose each day,
Knowing that new adventures were on the way.
The future was upon us; it has started now,
We must deal with this reality; I know we can, somehow.

The summer came and went; we started a new life,
Wondering if this adventure was a double edge knife.
"Ready, get set, go," was our battle cry to be,
Two people testing new waters; that was you and me.

Our Drummer's Beat

We bought our new boat; we are now in one home,
God has blessed us dearly, as we move forward on our own.
The water under our keel, as the time slips away,
The memories of it all will be with us every single day.

As fall became winter, and our circle came complete,
The 12th of January will mark the beginning of our drummer's beat.
Many questioned our wisdom and thought as we marched to what
we heard,
"A Greek Jewish Lady and a Texas Christian Man," we were not
disturbed.

The sun will never set on the Twelfth of Never; this is what is to be,
We felt in our hearts and souls, this is the life for you and me.
I pray for many more twelfths, may they last forever,
And I know they will as long as you and I are together.

OUR FIRST BOAT

OUR HORIZONS

Our adventures come from both near and far,
And our guiding light is a wandering star.
Each day is a blessing as we go on our way,
Toward each new horizon, come what may.

We are now looking to bringing our boat home,
A boat that is ours, together we own.
This is the first of many days ahead,
As we grow together, anchors away, less said.

Now we move on, looking for the day,
As Mr. and Mrs. C, and we will do it our way.
Hazy tomorrows will come, but one thing is clear,
That this is a love that will last year after year.

Thanks for each day that brings me much joy,
You made me so happy, yeah, this little boy.
I did not think it would happen, this joy so great,
We have started a new story, I am ready, can't wait.

Counting Our Blessings

There was this trip we took, and we can only explain,
If we knew what we were doing, we must have been insane.
With a few bags, our golf clubs, our hat, and our coat,
We left in a car and came back in a boat.

That time we were together, on the land and the sea,
Brought us together as one, from now until eternity.
God made this happen; this is something we could not guess,
We made our decision to go as one, and God did bless.

Each day is a blessing, each day a new dawn,
And now and forever, we gladly move on.
This is our commitment, to love each other more each day,
And counting our blessings as we go along our way.

If we are together, nothing can break us apart,
And nothing is stronger than love from a heart.
We are bound as one, so let all who doubt see,
That true love and happiness glows from you and me.

BOAT'S FIRST BIRTHDAY

Nineteen months together, is already here,
And now our Baby Puddin' is approaching one year.
She took us many miles, while helping bond our love,
With our commitment to each other and guidance from above.

We started as different entities, thinking that this is what is to be,
But by the grace of God, it became one, which is you and me.
The time has gone by with a joy that we want to last forever,
And we have been blessed with this love and the Twelfth of Never.

We move on each day with joy, love, and trust,
You, me, and our Baby Puddin', this is a must.
Each day is an adventure, each day a treat,
Never knowing over each horizon, what we will meet.

The horizons in front of us, or as far as the ones behind,
What we live for is now, and it is yours and mine.
Each day a new beginning, or the continuing of the day before,
But no matter how it develops, I keep loving you more and more.

Now that our summer here is coming to an end,
We can start thinking of the future, you, me, and Puddin',
Happy birthday to our great boat, may many more come,
May our love for each other, keep us all as one

New Starts

Each day of the season will start as the one before,
The sun will rise, dare we ask for more.
The blessings that we have that each morning will bring,
It makes us want to sing out loud, it causes a church bell to ring.

These days of the season are the one that make us look inside our heart,
And give thanks for everything, even making new starts.
Thanksgiving, Christmas, and Hanukkah, all a part of this time,
And we can go into it, knowing that I am yours and you are mine.

We travel the roads, seeing our family and friends,
Knowing that returning to our home is a beginning, not an end.
We will travel the waterways, enjoying what God gave us to share,
Our love for each other, our love for the open air.

Every day is a building block that will make our love strong,
With this in our hearts, nothing will go wrong.
For the only thing that matters is the love between you and me,
Everything else that happens will be easy as one, two, three.

Season and Time for Joy

When does time start for the beginning of the day,
When does the flower start, when does it fade away?
As the flower of our lives grows from the bud to the end,
We will enjoy the time we are given, never stopping before we begin.

Twenty-three months in the making, our love continues to shine,
Each day is a blessing given to us, let us treat is like a fine wine.
To age, nourish, and enjoy until the last drop is gone,
This is our quest for life, and we will go all the way with a song.

We have grown together as one, never doubting our choice,
All can see it in our faces; they can hear it in our voice.
This is the season for joy, we will make the most of our time,
Starting a new life together, that is only yours and mine.

This season will come and go, as the sun in the sky,
But we know each day is a beginning, and never ask why.
For we know that our love is strong, and we will conquer all fears,
And we will go together as one through all the coming years.

CHAPTER 3

2015

Two Years Together

There is this time, the time that we live
We can choose to take, or choose to give.
Love is a mysterious item, something not to deceive,
For if you are always giving it, you will always receive.

Our moments turned to days, then weeks, then years,
And as time passed by, our horizon became truly clear.
We moved together as one, and with each passing day,
This is what we wanted for our lives, as we went on our way.

It seems that I have always known you, like we have never been apart.
Always moving together, never having to stop, never having to start.
Now that our year has become two, and we break from life's cage,
We know what we want for this act, as we play it out on our stage.

As we get closer to our day, to be joined as one,
I think of all the times under the moon and the sun.
If I am happy, lucky, and blessed, forget any roll of the dice.
For I had one great year, and then it became twice.

VALENTINE TODAY,
WIFE TOMORROW

Twenty-five months have passed, and February is here,
It is Valentine's month, and we have started another year.
It is closer to our wedding with the passing of each day,
For in our hearts is total love, and the rest is come what may.

Each day we are together, and no one can explain it away,
That whatever we have together is here forever to stay.
Never has this feeling consumed me to this degree,
The blessings are coming together; this is what will be.

Your kisses, your hugs, your touch are the reasons for this great life,
And it is only going to get better when we start as husband and wife.
A little more time to go for our next journey to begin,
When we start the race of our life, with one goal—to win.

Love and happiness in our hearts is all the fuel we need,
To make this life be the best, let all others take heed.
We know our paths to travel, and we are going all the way,
So our advice to anyone in front of us—lead, follow, or get out of
our way.

MARCH 12 CEREMONY

There comes a time in two people's lives that is quite different from any other experience they may ever have. This is the bonding of their hearts, their bodies, and their souls. They become as one body and live as one, sharing their lives with each other and holding dear that incredibly special trust. In other words, falling in love.

Tom and Nancy have experienced this special feeling in hearts and commitment to each other and want to profess before all that they want to continue their lives as Mr. and Mrs. Campbell.

Some have wondered if Tom and Nancy, who are from quite different cultures and backgrounds and are at this point in life, should try to make this union happen. Can anything good come from this union? They are like hydrogen and oxygen, two very explosive elements; but when combined, they will form water. This is the basis of all life as we know it. There is the difference between day and night that seems so opposite, yet the world could not exist without an equal balance of both. Love makes life complete. Love has no boundaries—love has no clock. Love cannot be bought or sold. Love can only be given and accepted. Love is not just a feeling, but also a way of life. When two people are in love, they think as one and they move as one. Tom and Nancy wants everyone to know—that this is how they feel toward each other.

Their lives have crossed, and they want to continue as one in life's journey. This journey will make them happy and complete. The chain of events and the timing of their meeting have been deemed by Tom and Nancy as a sign that this union is blessed by God, and they want to honor this blessing. So from today on, these two will be bonded in holy matrimony.

OUR WEDDING POEM

They say that a long life and happiness come from many sources,
Like older whiskey, younger women, and faster horses.
Gambling is not my game, and age is just a number,
But the spirits of my bar, I have been known to plunder.

You came into my life, and slowly we became as one,
We made a commitment to each other, and we have only just begun.
There will be mountains to cross and storms to weather,
But all can be conquered, as long as we are together.

You are my best friend next door, the wild child across the street,
You are the mysterious face in the crowd that I would like to meet.
You are everything that is good for me, everything that brings me life,
That why it makes me feel great, by taking you for my wife.

There will be times that I stumble and fall to my knee,
If you cannot pick me up, just lay down beside me.
We go as a team, never wanting to part,
Now and forever, and this is our start.
I love you,
Your loving captain and husband

Charting Our Course

Now that we have started a whole new life,
By me taking you for my wife,
We will continue as we have done before,
With our hearts tied together and much more.

We will walk in the sunlight; we are together each night,
Knowing that all we do, we are doing it right.
For our one body, one soul, now commanded by one source,
Like a sailboat on the sea, sails trimmed, one course.

One month into our marriage, many more to come,
Each one is a blessing, and our love will never be done.
For each is greater than the one before,
As each day we demand nothing, but we get more.

April showers bring May flowers, as an old poem said,
But it will be the catalyst for our love to grow instead.
Never knowing what lies ahead, whether sorrow or fun,
We know we have each other, and we always go as one.

Going Forward

It was about two years ago in the month of May,
I took you to Texas to tell all that you were here to stay.
Now we are married to each other, our first summer as one,
To continue our life together, and now we have just begun.

We have our home, our boat, our health, and our love,
We go and do together with the blessing from above,
Never fearing or looking back, for we know all is right,
And we will approach all challenges with all our might.

The continuing of our life is ahead of us, the past has set in the West,
For each morning we wake together, knowing that this is the best.
Each day is a blessing, to have you by my side,
Whether we are on an adventure, or where we abide.

Holding you each morning, as the sun gives light to the sky,
I know that I have been blessed by God, and do not ask why.
For what I feel in my heart, and as it grows every day,
Is only something that comes from above, what else can I say?

God's Amazing Grace

When our worlds came together, all the angels did sing,
Knowing that our strength's together, good things to the world, we
would bring.
Loving and laughing, sometimes casting our fate to the wind,
And this strength and love is the bond that will never bend.

People see us together with a smile on our face,
Since each day for us is the results of God's Amazing Grace.
He blessed us with our love that we cherish always so dear,
And it will keep us so strong, all through the rest of our years.

We planned our wedding, our honeymoon, and life,
And we will continue this path as husband and wife.
Whether it is an anchorage near home, or trips to a foreign land,
We know that we can do it, walking hand in hand.

We are on our way now to many new things,
With our love and devotion, we can handle what life brings,
The wedding celebration is over, and friends and family went away,
But for you and me always, our happiness stays as a permanent wed-
ding day.

A Moment in Time

Time is just a measurement of things in the past,
Or it could be the future, hoping all things will last.
We live in each moment, knowing that our love was to be,
Cherishing each of those moments, when it is just you and me.

Time has flown by since we first met,
And what it has grown to and become, no one would bet.
That this love that we have is timeless as the sky,
And six months of marriage, we are still riding high.

We are always one as the clock ticks away,
If that is our motto, then tomorrow is just another day.
We look at each other with love in our heart,
Each day is a blessing, and nothing will tear us apart.

The things we acquire over time will come and go,
But the love I have for you, I hope you will always know,
That it is here forever, and with the passing of time,
My life will always be complete, as long as you are mine.

Birthday Wishes

We are brought into this life and taken down a rode,
And we start the journey not knowing our mode.
Each day can be an adventure, with blessings or trials,
But we carry on our best, only resting for a while.

With all the issues that can govern our day,
We never want to lose sight as we make our way.
For the days may be many, with memories that may blur,
But there is always the day that we all can concur.

The day of our birth is a day that is special to all,
Whether we speed down the road, or move with a crawl.
Your birthday is special to me since it started you on the trail,
That crossed the path of my journey, not knowing what would unveil.

Happy birthday, my love. May we get to celebrate many more,
Together on this special day, and many other days to explore.
For as old as you are, and as old as you get to be,
As long as we are together, you are the only one for me.

THINKING OF OUR LOVE
AT THANKSGIVING

Today came to an end and turned into night,
And I look to you, the one to be my guiding light.
Whether near or far, your body may abide,
I know, soon, that you will be by my side.

We have grown together as one, as a river to a sea,
Never growing apart, never doubting, that is you and me.
For when I watch you sleep, or as we walk, holding hands,
Our love is never ending, as the shore beaches and all the sand.

Eight months have passed since we took our vows,
And I love you more today, I did not think I knew how.
And this is the month, of Thanksgiving we will share,
With our friends and family, there will be love in the air.

The day is there for us as we go,
Through life as one, we will let anyone know,
That our love is real, and it grows each day,
If it is not obvious to all, then, what can I say?

THANKSGIVING PRAYER

I am thankful when I get to look into your eyes,
I am thankful when you get me a little surprise.
I am thankful for each day when we wake and then,
I am thankful that we get to start our day over again.

Knowing and loving you has made my life complete,
Each day is a blessing; each day is a treat.
Sharing our love and the blessings that have come our way,
I want to wish you our first Happy Thanksgiving on this glorious
day.

CHAPTER 4

2016

British Isles Trip

We made a little trip around the British Isles, including the Channel Islands, in the summer of 2016 as pointed out in my little story of our exploits in that year. I found my family war crest (shown in a previous picture when I was on the balcony of our room on the Queen Elizabeth), a Campbell Clan Calder plaid shawl. But I could not find a tartan flat cap with the Campbell Clan Calder plaid to replace the one that I was wearing with another clan plaid. And I refused to purchase a Scottish kilt. I think I saw the Loch Ness monster poke his head out of the water and say, "Do not tell anyone I am here." At least it appeared that way through the bottom of my scotch glass as we had a little happy hour in honor of Nessie.

ANOTHER YEAR, ANOTHER DAY—GOOD MORNING

A new year is beginning, and we know not what lies ahead,
We walk together in harmony, never fearing, never to dread.
For all that reality will bring us, it will be a part of our life,
We will take each step as one, never parting, conquering all strife.

Today is our reality, tomorrow is our dream,
Yesterday is the past; our souls are clean.
This journey started with a blessing from God,
And some thought our combo was at best, a little odd.

Each day I wake to the sound of your voice,
And I say, "Good morning, Miss Puddin'," and I still like my choice.
For you are the one that makes me want to sing
Every love song there is that make a heart ring.

Now that we are making our lives as one,
No matter how far we travel, whether walking or on the run.
I know I will love you tomorrow, more than the day before,
And I promise to make you happy, so let us proceed to explore.

Defining Our Twelfth
of Never

Never in my life has it been so clear
That all has been right for this past year.
Just knowing that our love is something that is forever,
And our wedding day started our Twelfth of Never

Who would have guessed that the words of a song
Would be something in my heart, all day long.
To me these words are special and will never die
If the ground is below us, and up above us, is the sky.

You ask how much I need you, must I explain,
I need you, oh my darling, like roses need rain.
You ask how long I'll love you. I'll tell you too,
Until the Twelfth of Never, I'll still be loving you.

These words are real, and they come from my heart,
They will keep us together, and we will never part
You are part of my body, my heart, and my soul,
And finally in my life, you have made me whole.

May our life together be as bright as a rose,
Proving to us and others it is right, what we chose.
To spend our days together for all to see,
That our marriage is blessed for now and eternity.

Taking Me to New York

It started when you asked me to go
On a trip to New York, and who would know,
It began a new life that will last forever,
And we would grow up with our Baby Puddin', that is the Twelfth
of Never.

A simple little trip to your home by Long Island Sound,
Was the recipe to make my heart go round and round.
The little things we did, to the big decisions we made,
Was it a stroke of luck, or a hand well played?

We walked on Glen Island, we chatted with that little man,
Maybe all of this was the beginning part of God's plan.
Our time at the Italian restaurant, our drives through the countryside,
Put what we have all together, and it is strong and sure as the tide.

We have traveled many places, and there is much more to see,
Whether it is land, sea, or the air, it is always you and me.
The best part of all, is the love that is ours to share,
For this is the greatest, to which nothing can compare.

Our Show—No Matter Where the Stage

Was it you, or was it me, I do not know,
Who created the lines of our great show?
Maybe they were created in the heavens above,
And all we must do is perform them with love.

It has been said, I heard someone say on a bus,
That life is a stage, and the actors are us.
We say our lines, we perform our part,
Knowing that this is no act, it comes from the heart.

Our country's birthday, and we will be around the spot
Where my roots begin, maybe yes, maybe not.
For my life began the day I fell in love with you.
We were sailing alone on an ocean so blue.

The crossing of our courses, or the raising of a curtain
Put our future on a destiny that was to be certain.
Whether it is a direction to a place of a performance in life,
I am so glad that the results made you become my wife.

Revisiting the Past—
Looking Forward

The end of the summer is on its way,
From Key Largo to the Frisco Bay.
The month of September marks the beginning of our life,
Which led to the day when you became my wife.

We started a trip, as we brought our new boat home,
And now the completion of the trip where the buffalo roam.
We have covered this great country from the east to the west,
And I knew from the beginning that I was with the best.

No matter where we go, on land, air, or the sea,
Nothing is better than when it is just you and me.
The final leg of this trip is about to begin,
Where it started a while back, where I started to win.

And each trip is a reminder of how lucky we are,
Whether it is on land, or sea, or just looking at a star,
To be able to have these many trips, as many as we can plan,
And they can take us from the mountains of Switzerland, to the Rio
Grande.

As each trip ends, a new one will begin,
And there is always that something that pounds from within.
Love is a blessing, that makes our lives strong,
And we will cherish each day together while our lives go on.

BIRTHDAY WISH

I wake up each morning, and what do I see,
The wonderful union, of just you and me.
I must pause for a second while I make a sigh,
Oh, what the heck. Good morning, howdy, and hi!

Never knowing in life, what will come our way,
But we have our love to bless us every single day.
Each day is the greatest that starts with a kiss
This is something I treasure; without it, I would miss.

The clicking of the clock, the rise and setting of the sun,
For us, the only time is time to walk, or time to run.
God put us together to go forward at our pace,
We can go fast or slow, this is only our race.

By order of the clock, as our days together become more,
Each day once a year, it is the rule to keep score.
Add a year to your age, so the prophets have said,
And you make a wish over your cake, who knows what is ahead.

This we cannot know, for the future is never here,
It is something we look toward and should never fear.
Our hearts will always be young, and our souls without time,
And the life and love we have together will make the church bell
chime.

SIXTY-EIGHTH BIRTHDAY

The day of your birth has come, and it was my lucky day,
Because it brought you to my life as I was making my way.
All journeys seem to have a beginning and an end,
But this journey has found me with love and a best friend.

There will be many rivers to cross and mountains to climb,
Through many years of counting the numbers, it is just time.
For time we cannot stop, it will come as fast as it goes,
When time stops for anyone, no one really knows.

This is your day, may all your wishes come true,
Mine already have, when it is just me and you.
Happy birthday, my Puddin', many more of these days to come,
And no matter what is your number, you will always be my number
one.

LOOKING FORWARD TO
THE FESTIVE HOLIDAYS

Nineteen months since our day of coming together,
I knew from the start that there would be no other.
For you were the one that set my heart ablaze,
It was like I was walking in a mysterious daze.

Now we are approaching the festive season,
Gives me cause to write for many of reasons.
For with you I have prospered in the greatest of ways,
Never wanting for anything, what can I say?

I wish these months could have been years,
With us together, making a life, conquering all fears.
But God saw it to be the way it has come,
As we make up for the time, and we have just begun.

Thanksgiving, Christmas, Hanukkah, and more
Will round out the year, and then onward to explore.
There are mountains to climb, and rivers to cross,
But with our love and devotion, we will just give fate a toss.

CHAPTER 5

2017

EXOTIC TRAVEL

The end of the year has come and gone,
As we dwell on the things that we came upon.
Never in my life have I seen so much,
From the beauty of this world to your loving touch.

I have experienced many things that I thought were out of reach,
From the Panama Canal to Scotland, and all it would teach.
With all the world's blessings that are sent from above,
The best part was sharing these things with the one that I love.

Never in my life would I embark with such zest,
And it has to do with the one thing that I love best.
For the beauties of the world, with its wonders and lures,
Do not outshine my Puddin', with your love so pure.

You are the real thing that matters in my life,
And that is why I asked you to be my wife.
No matter what treasures the world can provide,
Nothing is better than having you by my side.

BEING ON THE SAME PAGE

Our vacation is over, and we are headed south,
It was an awesome experience, well, shut my mouth.
Going anywhere with you is the wind in my sail,
And that is what is great, together anywhere, whatever it will entail.

We discovered new territory, we saw different horizons,
Each day with you never stops being so surprising.
We walk and talk; we hold each other's hand,
And our future is out there for whatever God will command.

We count our blessings, thanking God for his grace,
And I count mine especially, each time I see your beautiful face.
How I got so lucky to have you by my side,
As my wife, lover, and best friend, you will always be my bride.

As each day passes to see what comes our way,
We will take it in stride together, and will never sway.
The music to our love is playing, that we are on the same page,
And this is our song, our dance, and we are on the stage.

YOU AND ME

Time goes on, and it cannot be stopped,
It is a fact for all, from the bottom to the top.
Our time began on one beautiful day,
And then God guided us along the way.

We did not know, if by chance, when we met,
Was it something to remember, or to forget?
Not knowing the future is the way it will be,
But our future was sealed, it is you and me.

I thank God for each day, for my time with you,
And we will enjoy our time together, this is true.
So as the time marches on, and each moment is new,
Traveling the earth together, that will be me and you.

FOUNDATION OF A TRUE COURSE

It is a fact, and the realities of life are shown,
It can make us pause to reflect about our own.
Each moment can be a lifetime; we enjoy each one.
Each day a new beginning, we have only just begun.

Thirty-one months as my wife, I wish it would have been years,
And though time is just a measurement, my happiness should be
clear.
For inside and out, I feel a radiation of joy and love,
And each day I am thankful for this gift sent from above

We should never think of a day as something in our past,
But part of the foundation that will make us last.
This is the foundation we stand on, our love, our respect, our trust,
And we use each other for strength, as always, we must.

We go into our future, knowing only that our love is real,
This is our compass; this is what gives us the will.
There will be battles to conquer, and there will be stormy weather,
But we will survive it all if we hold our course, and that will keep us
together.

LAST YEAR OF THE SIXTIES

This is the day, the month that starts your last year,
Of this decade of numbers, and let me make this clear,
That you will always be my girl of twenty that makes me feel alive,
And I will always have that great feeling as if I were twenty-five.

I sometimes wonder what I was doing, the day you came into this
world,
Was I riding my tricycle, coloring in a book, or even thinking how a
sail is to be furled?
None of this will matter since our trails now have crossed,
And all the elements that kept us apart have now been tossed.

This day will be the start as your last year of the sixties,
And your zest for life and excitement would inspire a band of gypsies.
Enjoy this day, this year, and I pray to God in Heaven
That he will bless and keep you to the days that you age starts with
a seven,

Year Ending, Future Steps Beginning

December has come to end another year,
And we can count our blessings and give a cheer.
For what we have, for these three hundred and sixty-five days,
Is a true gift from God, and we are both amazed.

As the start of the year is just another day,
Is the ending the results of something we cannot explain away?
Never could I want for more, than to have you in my life,
As my best friend, my navigator, my lover, and my wife.

We will aim high on every journey we take,
To enjoy everything to the fullest, nothing is fake.
Our love is real, just as the sky is blue,
And nothing can stop us, the love team of me and you.

The Christmas season and Hanukkah too,
We will enjoy our friends and family, and consume a little brew,
Since we have started in motion a new direction for next year,
The future steps we take, we do together and without fear.

CHAPTER 6

2018

Boat Gone or Moving On

This is the month that will bring us much change,
And most of the items, we did arrange.
As we start this month with our boat gone away,
And we are looking for another to continue our play.

Our adventures may be extended to waters we have not seen,
But the only thing that matters is that I will be with my queen.
We can share the times and enjoy all this beautiful land,
And whatever trouble comes our way, we will overcome it hand in
hand.

As we go forward, knowing that this is what we want to do,
Each decision will be made, even if we think we do not have a clue.
For our experience has taught us, and guided us to where we are,
And nobody or nothing can keep us, from aiming for our star.

For when our paths crossed, and others wanted us to sway,
The love we felt in our hearts told us to go our own way.
We look, we love, and we do what others seem to have forgot,
When others asked why you are doing this, we just asked "Why not?"

SEARCHING FOR A NEW BOAT

We travel our path, and now it is June,
And good things are happening, and not too soon.
We looked and searched for a time that seems forever,
To find a new addition to our lives, another Twelfth of Never.

We did our due diligence, and now we are ready to go,
I know we are moving fast, but sometimes it seems slow.
It is times like these that create the bonds of our love,
And the compass we follow guides us from above.

Never feel weary, for our love is strong,
And if we are together, what could go wrong.
I know I am optimistic, but you make me that way,
And since I have you, we will continue to play.

Life is an adventure, life is a trip,
And each step we take, we will do like a crack of a whip.
We will follow our menu, and here is what we will say,
"Here we come, and we are doing it our way."

A Team Forever

For many months now that have turned into years,
We have loved and laughed; we have also had tears.
New life and joys have blessed us as they have come our way.
While some loved ones have departed to be with another day.

While life is a journey, full of curves and obstacles to pass,
We will always approach our life as the water half full in our glass.
Attacking all matters together, it is not "just you" or not "just me."
But we are a team forever, as our years of anniversaries come to three.

Each day is a blessing, and I always thank my lucky star,
For that day that I stumbled by you standing by your car.
It was a new beginning for my life, one that I could not dream,
Travel, adventure, and love, this will always be our theme.

Whether we walk down the block, or travels to corners of the world,
We will make our plans with our sails totally unfurled.
And knowing what is right for us, no one can make us sway,
For the decisions we make for us is us doing it our way.

New Bern, North Carolina

As a few of the previous lines of rhyme have **all**uded to, we were in search of a new boat. After several months of looking, we final found the one we wanted in New Bern, North Carolina. We were there several months and had to endure all the problems that were associated with Hurricane Florence and Hurricane Michael. Fortunately for us, prior to the storms, we were able to photograph some of more than fifty fiberglass bears in and around the city that are beautifully decorated. If you get a chance to go to New Bern, check them out.

A Few of the Bears in New Bern, North Carolina

STUMBLED IN

Our love is alive, so let it begin,
The words of a song that seems to make us grin.
Who could have known that my little stroll one day
Could have brought us to this point, what can I say?

We have been over this country with more to come,
And some parts of the world, can you hear the beat of our drum?
I put my heart on the table; I held nothing back,
I was on a course of uncertainty, but you made me change my tack.

We are now in search for a new adventure to start,
We plan, we think, we act, we go together—not apart.
Whatever happens in the future, we will have done our best
To make our adventures an experience, and not a test.

The difference between adventure and ordeal is attitude,
And this is the way we want to keep it, no matter our latitude or
longitude.
So as the new adventure is about to begin,
I will always be thankful for the day when I stumbled in.

Discovering Each Other

A summer started four years ago,
When you said, "There is this place I want you to go.
To see where I am from, and learn about me,
For all these things, I want you to see."

This was the beginning of what is now our life,
With a love so strong, it cannot be separated with a knife.
The beginning may have had questions, needless to say,
But God put us together, and then come what may.

We have traveled together, by land, air, and sea,
Becoming as one.
Now we continue, and our life goes on,
Enjoying each day, for whatever we come upon.

Life is a journey, as many have said,
The destination is not important, but the trip instead.
When our trip is over, only God knows when,
But until then, each of our journeys is for us to begin.

SECOND TWELFTH OF NEVER

We thought, we planned, we searched for what was right,
We negotiated, we prayed until all the concepts were in sight.
Now we have it after being prudent and clever,
And we are starting another adventure on our next Twelfth of Never.

But this is just a medium that moves us along,
And it keeps us close together, as we continue to sing our song.
Whether it is "Stumbling In" or the lyrics to our boat's name,
Being always together, we do nothing in vain.

Some storms may come, and the reefs will appear,
But we will overcome and continue with a cheer,
Our course may vary, our destination may change,
For wherever we are is our home on the range.

Independence Day is here, and we wish our country the best,
Happy birthday, America; we too, have been blessed.
And may the greatness of our country be transformed to our life,
As we take on our new adventure as a happy and loving husband and
wife.

OUR SECOND TWELFTH OF NEVER

STRIDING THE HURDLES

When you walk a bumpy road, it is better to step lightly.
If a curve slows you down, cautiously speed up slightly.
Our life is a journey, and wherever we go,
We will do it together, be it fast or be it slow.

We will take each hurdle in stride, no matter what the test.
Each one is our focus, and we will do the rest.
The task will always be ours, as we face it as a team,
Conquering all in front of us, even as difficult as it may seem.

The difficulties behind us are over, but more will surely arrive,
But the team that is together is the team that will survive.
It is our love that is our bond that will give us our strength,
And we will overcome and go to any length.

As summer turns to fall, and we prepare for the miles ahead,
We will get the Twelfth of Never ready to repeat the miles we have
tread.
For wherever our adventures deliver us, near, far, or standing still,
Our love will show us the way along with God's will.

The "Big Easy" Birthday

The road of life makes many turns, and goes on and on,
Some of the challenges we know are coming, some we stumble upon.
Never knowing any outcome, for the future is just a step away,
So we will handle any situation, and not worry about what they say.

We are a team; we are an army—let no one think that is not true.
And each victory is our happiness, and it only takes me and you.
On this path of life, it is certain that there will be things that we lack,
But the one thing that we will always have is that we have each other's
back.

Our life started when you were almost three scores and five years,
We have gone through many adventures; we shared a few tears.
Our blessings are many, and as the years go by,
We will continue to thank God that he put the team together called
"You and I."

Now is the time for another birthday celebration, that start of another
decade,
And remember that seven zero is just a number in another escapade.
You have the envy of many, and the respect of many more,
But the love, all that know you, is too immense to explore.

This place of celebration is where we made our first trip,
And if it is a full-blown exploration, or just a small clip,
We will cherish our times in the Big Easy,
Eating gumbo, having a riverboat ride, or just doing something sleazy.

Happy birthday, my love, with many more to come,
And at eighty, ninety, and one hundred, you will still be my sugarplum.
You are the one thing in my life that I will cherish all my life,
And the smartest thing I ever did was ask you to be my wife.

December Cheers

This month brings us to the end of the year,
As we go about greeting and spreading good cheer.
We know that this is the season that is the time to share our love
With those that count most in our lives, and to God above.

Happiness to each person may come in many ways,
From the smallest gift as a child, to having your heart set ablaze.
Happiness comes from the inside and is shown all about,
It will make you smile; it will make you shout.

I absolutely love you; my voice rings from the mountain high above.
May all hear these words, the words in my heart, the words of love.
There is no greater season that this joy should be shared,
As each Hanukkah and Christmas season comes, which no other can
be compared.

My love for you is every day of the year.
It grows more each day, and I want all to hear,
That I thank God for this present, which is the greatest of all,
Love and happiness, all rolled up in one beautiful ball.

CHRISTMAS TREE AT JEKYLL ISLAND

CHAPTER 7

2019

WISHES COME TRUE

When you wish upon a star,
Do you wonder, *Can a wish go that far?*
I guess it would travel toward that light,
And say all the time, "I think I can, I think I might."

Does the star come toward the wish as if to say
"What if I were to meet you about halfway?"
The wish and star, they will do what they do,
And their coming together, caused an "I love you."

That night on the pier, as we gazed into the sky,
I must have wished for something as the breeze blew by.
I saw your face with a look I had not seen,
And I knew from that moment, I wanted you for my queen.

To be your Jiminy Cricket, your leprechaun and more,
Your captain, your lover, your guide to explore.
But the best of all that could ever happen in my life
Is the wish that came true, and you are my wife.

On this Valentine's Day, which is month forty-seven,
I do believe this blessing was a gift from heaven.
Our life is one, no matter what comes our way,
And I will always love you, so enjoy this very special day.

LOOKING FOR A TANGIBLE

Three years have passed, and we are starting our number four,
And each day is a blessing as we continue our tour.
To walk a mile, or to fly many thousands,
To sail through each horizon, we continue our carousing.

As a child, I laid in the grass and looked up at the clouds,
Wondering what image would appear that would make me wow.
A horse with a rider, or a face of a president past,
But the wind came, and the image did not last.

I did not realize at that time in my life,
That I was looking for a tangible that would become my wife.
It took finding you, that made everything clear,
That the clouds come and go, but you are always here.

Our life together is a joy, every single day,
Whether we are solving the day's problems or at play.
We can look at the clouds together as they frolic along their way.
But we will hold strong because we are here to stay.

FOUR-YEAR ANNIVERSARY

Time will walk by, look back, and say,
"Are you coming with me, or do you intend to stay?"
The answer is certain, no matter what we think,
That our future is somewhere written in ink.

We think we know the answers; we try to carve a path,
Never knowing what is before us, never knowing when is the last breath,
The only thing that is for sure is what is in our hearts,
And this should be our compass as each sunrise gives our start.

The horizons behind me are the ones that I cannot see,
At best just a blur in a foggy memory.
My course is in front of me with you by my side,
And I am in it for the long run, no matter what the ride.

One day, was it luck, or was it by chance,
We met not knowing, this began our dance.
It did not take me long to know my heart wanted to say
That I wanted to be with you, every single day.

We have traveled some stormy seas, and they have gone away,
The gentle breezes always come, and we continue our play.
Whether it is storm or calm seas, through laughter and tears,
I am very proud and happy to be married to you for these four years.

THE TRAVELS OF TIME

We walk along a thorny path, not knowing what is ahead,
Should we take the step or make the turn, sometimes better, nothing said.
A look, a glance, a smile as we look into each other's eyes,
Maybe all we need for comfort as we search for clearer skies.

The path of life is not easy, as we have truly found,
But the steps we take together will keep us on a solid ground.
Our boat will rock in a storm, and there will be many storms to weather,
But the storms and paths we will conquer since we are together.

Sometimes our guard is down; sometimes we fail to see
That each storm may bring a flower, one for you and one for me.
We traveled long roads separately to where our courses crossed,
Then we charted our course together to never again be lost.

The storms of life, the travels of time; can our course prevail?
No one knows the answer; only our hearts will tell.
For in our heart is our love that blocks out the fears of life,
And all courses will be charted by us, the greatest husband and wife.

LEAVE BOAT FOR OTHER TRAVELS

That time of the year has come to an end,
When we stop one activity, and others will begin.
We prepare our boats for a storm that may come,
And be moored and at rest while they collect water scum.

These are things that make up our life.
We do it together, in harmony or strife.
We roll with the waves or take them head on,
Whatever it takes, no matter what we come upon.

We found each other, and in cadence we walk,
And we pledge that to each other, not just talk.
For our lives are one, and that seals our bond,
Whether we are here, or over the horizon and beyond.

We prepare for our journey that will take us away,
We will see new things, and we will stop and play.
This is a part of life that we want to do,
But it would have no meaning if I did not have you.

Going Along Our Way

We walk along the shore, and we look out to the sea
To visualize the images of life that are you and me.
The waves of life may come, in cadence or by surprise,
And we know our strength of love is there as we look into each other's
eyes.

Storms may show on the horizon, and the sails, we may have to reef,
But our journey will continue; this is the plan, this is our belief.
To walk hand and hand on a sunny day, or to weather an unplanned
storm,
This is our life together; this is the greatest, this is our norm.

It is true our compasses may vary on which way to go,
But our set and drift will always be the same, be it fast or slow.
We go on the same ship, or we walk the same road.
Wherever we go, it is together. This is our code.

We can look back at the rolling ocean as we clear the breakwater of
time,
And we know we did it together, and the rewards are yours and mine.
For our journey's end will only come as God's plan will have its way,
But we will harvest the gifts he gives as we go along our way.

OUR IMPOSSIBLE DREAM

We have traveled many miles; we have far to go
With each step together, be it fast or be it slow.
New horizons we have found, always as a team,
And we found it together, our impossible dream.

Our road, at times, will be difficult as we travel to the top
To keep moving forward, defying anyone who thinks we cannot.
We will always have each other, whether we go near or far,
And with our total love and bond, we will reach for the unreachable
star.

Nothing can stop us; there is nothing we cannot do,
No matter if it is on land, or the wide big blue.
Our bond is our strength; nothing will break that seal.
Of all the contracts in the world, ours is the best deal.

We are halfway through our journey for this summer of fun,
And each day brings me pleasure as if it had just begun.
Hold my hand and follow, or take me along the way,
Which comes first is not important as long as it is us today.

GOING TO ALASKA

The following photographs are from some of our views and exploits in Alaska on an Azamara cruise ship trip. It was a beautiful trip, and as you can see, shorts and T-shirts were not required in Alaska in July. I did not put into rhyme much about Alaska since I could not come up with many words that rhymed with the state that commands the name "the land of the midnight sun."

A Complete Road Trip

We traveled from the Sunshine State to the Lone Star State,
And to the State of the midnight sun.
Back to Texas, Tennessee, and up to the Big Apple,
And then back to where we begun.

This was the greatest trip; this was the greatest adventure,
And it made my birthday and Christmas the best.
These are the things that I want to do with you,
Whether it is for our pleasure, or it might be a test.

It did not take me long to realize you were the one
That I wanted to be with forever,
And if I ever go gaga and change my mind,
It will be after the Twelfth of Never.

There are some stormy clouds on the horizon
That may make us feel as if we are locked in a cage,
And if something knocks us down and closes our book,
We will just get up and turn the page.

The original Grand Ole Opry, Nashville, Tennessee

THE MAGIC BIRTHDAY

Summer has passed, and our future is clear,
Still loving and going, if not somewhere else, why not here.
Nothing says love like I want to be here with you,
And showing it every day, and wanting to be true.

Love is not just words or an object to hold,
But a feeling from inside that gives you wealth untold,
That once anchored in your heart, never goes away,
And it gives you strength to handle anything that may come our way.

It was just about a year ago, we looked forward to this day,
And you reached a magic birthday with maybe happiness or dismay.
The age is only a number to me; you are my two score and five years,
And I will always look at you this way, be it good times or tears.

We will continue to walk this path to the beat of our own drum,
And never let anyone come between us—no changes to what we have
become.
We do everything together, no giving in, just going with,
And to think anything else is just some ancient myth.

Happy birthday to you my love, with many more to come,
And I will always be there, whether it is snow, rain, or sun.
You are at the top of my pinnacle, the only important thing in my
life,
And may each birthday you have be happy. Thanks for being my
wife.

Illusions and Conclusions

If I look at a mirror, what do I see?
All the things that are behind me.
If I turn from this mirror and walk away,
Does the past come to me, or does it stay?

We know the answer, for mirrors can be an illusion
That can trick us all into forming the wrong conclusion.
The only thing important is being here and real,
And that is what our life is about, that is our deal.

For our deal is, and we want all to know,
That all mirrors are aside, and this is not a show.
We live our lives, and we move at our pace,
If someone is ahead of us, it is their race.

We give thanks for each day of our life,
And we will do it together, as husband and wife.
We thank God for our love, family, and friends,
For our wealth in many ways, to bountiful ends.

HANUKKAH AND CHRISTMAS

It is hard to believe that the time is here,
That we have come again, the end of another year.
The holiday season marks a special time it seems,
And we celebrate the joys of all God-given things.

The joys we can share that have been given to us
Can only be placed on our ledger sheet as a plus.
And we were raised with different thoughts of the season,
But Hanukkah and Christmas bring joys for a reason.

The rededication of a temple, or the birth of Christ
Give us reason in our hearts for joy, no matter how it is sliced.
And what is in our hearts was given with God's love,
For love has no religion or boundaries, it is sent from above.

Fifty-seven months, approaching five years,
The time we have been as one brings me joy and happy tears.
I cannot imagine a different kind of life,
And trudging through this journey without you as my wife.

As this year ends and 2020 begins,
We can step forward in our journeys with no sorrows, no chagrins,
We walk our path in comfort, knowing our strength is our love,
And I know that our joy is shared to all as if sent from the wings of
a dove.

CHAPTER 8

2020

Beginning a New Year 2020

The end of the year has come, and where does it go?
Each day seems like a pinnacle, and I do not know.
Did the days come and go or just stayed in our hearts?
As the music of our lives, is to be our message to start.

The end of the year is a day that is part of our lives
As each day is filled with happiness, and that is no surprise.
Since the happiness we have is giving all our love,
And I hope our message is felt by all as we live hand and glove.

We start a new year with hope, peace, and love for all,
With new adventures to come, we will try not to stall.
For whatever happens in the next three sixty-five,
The important thing is that we are together when we arrive.

We go forward, knowing that I am yours, and you are mine,
And that will be our strength going forward as we sing "Auld Lang
Syne."

THE MONTH OF LOVE

Here we are married at month number fifty-nine,
And it has arrived in the month we celebrate Saint Valentine.
For this is the month of love, flowers, and giving,
And for us, a continuation of all of that. It is great to be living.

We walk, we talk, we smile as we hold each other by the hand,
To travel the rest of this life together, no matter where we make our
stand.
Being together is our strength, the bond that makes us one,
And that bond is our love that grows with each rising of the sun.

I have known since I was a small child I had a longing for the sea,
Since I saw the movie "Kon-Tiki," maybe I was searching for you
and me.
You got there before me; in your youth, you felt the breeze,
While my latitude-longitude coordinates delayed me, I continued on
with ease.

When I came into the anchorage of our life, not knowing what was
there,
I sensed a magic around me; I was not sure what to declare.
Was it just something new, or a horizon that I finally crossed,
Possibly the end of a rainbow, but I knew I was not lost.

Since this is the month of love, I know how I want it to begin,
By giving you these words that I will always be yours to the end.
Each day together is a blessing, each year is divine,
And each sunrise and sunset together will always be yours and mine.

OUR FIFTH ANNIVERSARY

Who would have known those five years ago,
When we made our commitment for all to know?
Where our love would take us, how far is the sky?
Never regretting a moment as time goes by.

We have seen many things happen, some good, and some bad.
We have traveled the world with a love that is iron clad.
There has been the passing of family and friends as well,
And the beginning of life for some, there will be stories to tell.

What is important to us, as we celebrate the occasion of wood?
Is knowing that our love will be a monument in all the places we
stood.
From traveling on the water, or walking down a trail,
To waking each morning, our love has no scale.

Each day is a blessing, and we go together with no sorrow,
For as each day passes, we just say, "Hello, Tomorrow."
God gives us time, and God takes it away,
And we thank God for our time every single day.

I have been in love with you all of my life,
My voyage just had to cross yours for you to become my wife.
Now that we are one, and we are on our next five-year start,
I pledge my undying love again, not just words, but from the heart.

IS THERE TIME?

Is there time
To walk in the woods or to watch another sunset?
Is there time
To remember the things and ponder what we do not want to forget.

Remembering our first dance, or the first time I made you a meal,
Thinking of our first kiss, to me, was a big deal.
Our journeys, our talks, a cool breeze at anchor with a glass of wine,
These are the things we need to remember; is there time?

We never want to forget the things that brought us this far,
And forge this path together, and even wish upon a star.
The thorns of life will always be there to act as a sign
That life is not always easy. Can we make it? Is there time?

I see you each morning and all through the day,
We lay in bed each night; I hear you sleeping. Tomorrow we will play.
Time is only a measurement of things in the future or past,
But our love is endless, and we got to save the best for last.

The red sky in the morning can always appear at will,
Same as that sky at night can comfort and give us a thrill.
And being together as we are with one love that is yours and mine,
We will always know that is our strength, and yes, there is time.

Strength through Pandemic

All trails have crossroads—go left, go right, or continue straight ahead,
If you wish, you can stop or turn around instead.
The road may seem easy when you are looking from afar,
But the reality of life is different when you are living your own memoir.

Now is a time we have never had that is taking us on a different path,
And we are having to make decisions to get us through this or bring us wrath.
Whatever decisions we make that will take us to sunny skies,
We will be doing it together, and that will always be our prize.

For our union is our bond, and our bond is what makes us strong,
And for that, I will always feel we can never go wrong.
Each day is a blessing to have you by my side,
And life is always beautiful, no matter where we abide.

Loving and sharing our lives in good times and bad
Are the things that make me feel great like nothing I ever had.
So no matter which way we turn, or which decision we make,
It will be our decision to go on, and it will be our personal wake.

I love you and we will get through this terrible time in our world's history.

Maneuvering through Uncertainty

The path that we choose may not always be certain.
We walk out on the stage and wait for someone to open the curtain.
When we stand there alone, not knowing what we will see,
We know we must conquer it since it is our eternity.

We are now looking at paths, wondering which one to take,
And never knowing if the right recipe is baked into the cake.
We think we have it right, but an obstacle will appear.
Is it a mountain or a boulder; sometimes it is not clear?

If the path disappears, and we do not know the way,
And we are together; we can continue slowly or stay.
Sometimes a load gets too heavy, which may cloud our view,
And we might forget the important things are me and you.

The path is always there, all we must do is look,
And we will travel each page as one, since this is our book.
Whatever may get us down, cause a course change, or make us stop,
As long as we are together, that will get us to the top.

Thus having our love is the best guide for our life,
And we will cut through all obstacles, as with the sharpest knife.
Never fear the darkness; never fear an impossible dream,
And all will be conquered in time with confidence since we are a
team.

WORDS FOR A JOURNEY

I know most of you have sons, daughters, nephews, nieces, or just a child of a close friend that you may want to say a few things to as they get ready to leave the nest and go to whatever their future endeavors may be. Sometimes it may be hard to think of all the things you might want to say with all of your experiences. And there is a good chance that they will not remember all of your words that you gave to them. I wrote the poem "Journey," and gave it to my son when he graduated from high school. The words are simple, and I think that as he has gotten older, he probably appreciates them now more than the day I gave him the poem.

THE JOURNEY

Britton,

You have traveled a journey, from boyhood to man.
I can remember when I held you in the palm of my hand.

You can remember the times when life was just play,
And enjoying it over the next and every day.

Life offers many hidden turns that a child cannot make,
But for the man that is prepared, there is no barrier he cannot break.

Take all that you have learned, the good and the bad.
This will be your ammunition; it can make you happy or sad.

As your childhood life ends, and you start your new journey alone,
Remember what is right, for this will keep you strong.

So with the force and fury of a plunging knife,
Get ready to start the journey of the rest of your life.

I LOVE YOU, MY SON.
DAD

DANCE THE TIDES

Too many times, we stand aside and let the waters slip away
Till what we put off to tomorrow has now become today.
So do not sit upon the shoreline and say you are satisfied.
Choose to chance the rapids, and dare to dance with the tide.

Epilogue

Monthly I have written a poem, as regular as the tide.
And it made no difference, at any point, where we did abide.
True, some did not pass muster, and on the cutting floor they rest,
And as June 12, 2020, comes to an end, we tried to deliver our best.

The poems will continue, as my love for Nancy will do,
And I can collect a few words of rhyme together, possibly edition two.
I hope you enjoyed these words, maybe just a stanza or a theme.
If this is true, then it is good that you can see my dream.

As the moon controls the tides,
It will always come and go.
But our love is an eternal tide,
And our life will always glow.

About the Author

Tom Campbell has been a pleasure boater since 1970, and a licensed captain since 1983. While working as an engineer for engineering and construction company in Houston, Texas, he also spent much of his free time cruising on his boat in Galveston Bay and the Texas Coast. He made many trips to the Caribbean on charter boats and with friends who were already cruising. He also taught sailing for Annapolis Sailing School, did private charters, boat deliveries, and a few boat repossessions. With these experiences, he was able to provide the magazines *Cruising World* and *Latitudes and Attitudes* with articles of his adventures and lifestyle. As a little gift to his wife Nancy, he decided to write a poem each month to help remind them of their times together. As the poems collected over the years, they decided to publish them as a token of their love for each other and as a constant reminder of their life together.

CPSIA information can be obtained
at www.ICGtesting.com
Printed in the USA
LVHW070003190821
695592LV00025B/2445